The gymnasiad, or boxing match. A very short, but very curious epic poem. With the prolegomena of Scriblerus Tertius, and notes variorum.

Paul Whitehead

ECCO
PRINT EDITIONS

The gymnasiad, or boxing match. A very short, but very curious epic poem. With the prolegomena of Scriblerus Tertius, and notes variorum.
Whitehead, Paul
ESTCID: T035932
Reproduction from British Library
Anonymous. By Paul Whitehead. With a half-title.
London : printed for M. Cooper, 1744.
[2],33,[1]p. ; 4°

Eighteenth Century
Collections Online
Print Editions

Gale ECCO Print Editions

Relive history with *Eighteenth Century Collections Online*, now available in print for the independent historian and collector. This series includes the most significant English-language and foreign-language works printed in Great Britain during the eighteenth century, and is organized in seven different subject areas including literature and language; medicine, science, and technology; and religion and philosophy. The collection also includes thousands of important works from the Americas.

The eighteenth century has been called "The Age of Enlightenment." It was a period of rapid advance in print culture and publishing, in world exploration, and in the rapid growth of science and technology – all of which had a profound impact on the political and cultural landscape. At the end of the century the American Revolution, French Revolution and Industrial Revolution, perhaps three of the most significant events in modern history, set in motion developments that eventually dominated world political, economic, and social life.

In a groundbreaking effort, Gale initiated a revolution of its own: digitization of epic proportions to preserve these invaluable works in the largest online archive of its kind. Contributions from major world libraries constitute over 175,000 original printed works. Scanned images of the actual pages, rather than transcriptions, recreate the works *as they first appeared.*

Now for the first time, these high-quality digital scans of original works are available via print-on-demand, making them readily accessible to libraries, students, independent scholars, and readers of all ages.

For our initial release we have created seven robust collections to form one the world's most comprehensive catalogs of 18th century works.

Initial Gale ECCO Print Editions collections include:

History and Geography
Rich in titles on English life and social history, this collection spans the world as it was known to eighteenth-century historians and explorers. Titles include a wealth of travel accounts and diaries, histories of nations from throughout the world, and maps and charts of a world that was still being discovered. Students of the War of American Independence will find fascinating accounts from the British side of conflict.

Social Science

Delve into what it was like to live during the eighteenth century by reading the first-hand accounts of everyday people, including city dwellers and farmers, businessmen and bankers, artisans and merchants, artists and their patrons, politicians and their constituents. Original texts make the American, French, and Industrial revolutions vividly contemporary.

Medicine, Science and Technology

Medical theory and practice of the 1700s developed rapidly, as is evidenced by the extensive collection, which includes descriptions of diseases, their conditions, and treatments. Books on science and technology, agriculture, military technology, natural philosophy, even cookbooks, are all contained here.

Literature and Language

Western literary study flows out of eighteenth-century works by Alexander Pope, Daniel Defoe, Henry Fielding, Frances Burney, Denis Diderot, Johann Gottfried Herder, Johann Wolfgang von Goethe, and others. Experience the birth of the modern novel, or compare the development of language using dictionaries and grammar discourses.

Religion and Philosophy

The Age of Enlightenment profoundly enriched religious and philosophical understanding and continues to influence present-day thinking. Works collected here include masterpieces by David Hume, Immanuel Kant, and Jean-Jacques Rousseau, as well as religious sermons and moral debates on the issues of the day, such as the slave trade. The Age of Reason saw conflict between Protestantism and Catholicism transformed into one between faith and logic -- a debate that continues in the twenty-first century.

Law and Reference

This collection reveals the history of English common law and Empire law in a vastly changing world of British expansion. Dominating the legal field is the *Commentaries of the Law of England* by Sir William Blackstone, which first appeared in 1765. Reference works such as almanacs and catalogues continue to educate us by revealing the day-to-day workings of society.

Fine Arts

The eighteenth-century fascination with Greek and Roman antiquity followed the systematic excavation of the ruins at Pompeii and Herculaneum in southern Italy; and after 1750 a neoclassical style dominated all artistic fields. The titles here trace developments in mostly English-language works on painting, sculpture, architecture, music, theater, and other disciplines. Instructional works on musical instruments, catalogs of art objects, comic operas, and more are also included.

The BiblioLife Network

This project was made possible in part by the BiblioLife Network (BLN), a project aimed at addressing some of the huge challenges facing book preservationists around the world. The BLN includes libraries, library networks, archives, subject matter experts, online communities and library service providers. We believe every book ever published should be available as a high-quality print reproduction; printed on-demand anywhere in the world. This insures the ongoing accessibility of the content and helps generate sustainable revenue for the libraries and organizations that work to preserve these important materials.

The following book is in the "public domain" and represents an authentic reproduction of the text as printed by the original publisher. While we have attempted to accurately maintain the integrity of the original work, there are sometimes problems with the original work or the micro-film from which the books were digitized. This can result in minor errors in reproduction. Possible imperfections include missing and blurred pages, poor pictures, markings and other reproduction issues beyond our control. Because this work is culturally important, we have made it available as part of our commitment to protecting, preserving, and promoting the world's literature.

GUIDE TO FOLD-OUTS MAPS and OVERSIZED IMAGES

The book you are reading was digitized from microfilm captured over the past thirty to forty years. Years after the creation of the original microfilm, the book was converted to digital files and made available in an online database.

In an online database, page images do not need to conform to the size restrictions found in a printed book. When converting these images back into a printed bound book, the page sizes are standardized in ways that maintain the detail of the original. For large images, such as fold-out maps, the original page image is split into two or more pages

Guidelines used to determine how to split the page image follows:

• Some images are split vertically; large images require vertical and horizontal splits.
• For horizontal splits, the content is split left to right.
• For vertical splits, the content is split from top to bottom.
• For both vertical and horizontal splits, the image is processed from top left to bottom right.

THE
GYMNASIAD,
OR
BOXING MATCH.

A very fhort, but very curious

EPIC POEM.

WITH THE

PROLEGOMENA of *Scriblerus Tertius,*

AND

NOTES VARIORUM.

(Price One Shilling.)

THE
GYMNASIAD,
OR
BOXING MATCH.

A very short, but very curious

EPIC POEM.

WITH THE

PROLEGOMENA of *Scriblerus Tertius,*

AND

NOTES VARIORUM.

—— *Nos hæc novimus effe nihil.*   Mart.

LONDON:

Printed for M. Cooper, at the Globe in Pater-noster-
Row. 1744.

[Price One Shilling.]

———————————————————

TO THE

Moſt Puissant and Invincible

Mr. *JOHN BROUGHTON.*

HAD this Dedication been addreſs'd to ſome *Reverend Prelate,* or *Female Court Favourite,* to ſome *Blundering Stateſman,* or *Apoſtate Patriot,* I ſhould doubtleſs have launched into the higheſt Encomiums on *Public Spirit, Policy, Virtue, Piety,* &c. and like the reſt of my Brother Dedicators had moſt ſuccefsfully impos'd on their Vanity, by aſcribing to them Qualities they were utterly unacquainted with, by which Means I had prudently reap'd the Reward of a *Panegyriſt* from

my

my *Patron*, and, at the fame Time, fecur'd the Reputation of a *Satyriſt* with the *Public*.

But ſcorning theſe baſe Arts; I preſent the following Poem to you, unſway'd by either Flattery or Intereſt; ſince your Modeſty would defend you againſt the Poiſon of the one, and your known Oeconomy prevent an Author's Expectations of the other. I ſhall therefore only tell you, what *you really are*, and leave thoſe (whoſe Patrons are of the higher Claſs) to tell them what *they really are not*. But ſuch is the Depravity of human Nature, that every Compliment we beſtow on another, is too apt to be deemed a Satire on ourſelves; yet ſurely while I am praiſing the Strength of your Arm, no Politician can think it meant as a Reflection on the Weakneſs of his Head, or while I am juſtifying your Title to the Character of a *Man*, will any modern Petit-Maitre think it an Impeach-

ment

ment of his Affinity to that of its mimic Counterfeit, a *Monkey*.

Were I to attempt a Defcription of your Qualifications, I might juftly have Recourfe to the Majefty of *Agamemnon*, the Courage of *Achilles*, the Strength of *Ajax*, and the Wifdom of *Ulyffes* ; but as your own heroic Actions afford us the beft Mirror of your Merits, I fhall leave the Reader to view in that the amazing Luftre of a Character, a few Traits of which only, the following Poem was intended to difplay ; and in which had the Ability of the Poet, equal'd the Magnanimity of his Hero, I doubt not but the GYMNASIAD had, like the immortal ILIAD, been handed down to the Admiration of all Pofterity.

As your fuperior Merits contributed towards raifing you to the Dignities you now enjoy, and plac'd you even as the SAFE-GUARD of Royalty itfelf,

felf, fo I cannot help thinking it happy for the Prince, that he is now able to boaft one *real* Champion in his Service: And what *Frenchman* would not tremble more at the puiffant Arm of a BROUGHTON, than at the ceremonious Gauntlet of a DIMMACK.

I am,

 with the moft profound Refpect

  to your HEROIC VIRTUES,

   your moft devoted,

    moft obedient,

     and moft humble Servant.

SCRIBLERUS TERTIUS

OF THE

P O E M.

IT is an old Saying that *Neceffity is the Mother of Invention*; it fhould feem then that Poetry, which is a *Species* of Invention, muft naturally derive it's Being from the fame Origin, hence it will be eafy to account for the many flimfy Ghoft-like Apparations, that every Day make their Appearance among us, for if it be true as Naturalifts obferve, that the Health and Vigour of the Mother is neceffary to produce the like Qualities in the Child, what Iffue can be expected from the Womb of fo *meagre a Parent*.

But there is another *Species* of Poetry, which inftead of owing it's Birth to the *Belly*, like *Minerva*, fprings at once from the *Head*, of this Kind are thofe Productions of Wit, Senfe, and Spirit, which once born, like the Goddefs herfelf immediately

ately becomes immortal. It is true these are a Sort of miraculous Birds, and therefore it is no Wonder they should be found so rare among us — As Glory is the noble Inspirer of the latter, so Hunger is the natural Incentive of the former, thus *Fame* and *Food* are the Spurs with which every Poet mounts his *Pegasus*, but as the Impetus of the *Belly* is apt to be more cogent than that of the *Head*, so you will ever see the one pricking and goading it in'd Jade to a hobbling Trot, while the other only incites the foaming Steed to a majestic Capriol.

The gentle Reader, it is apprehended will not long be at a Loss to determine, which *Species* the following Production ought to be rank'd under, but as the Parent most unnaturally cast it out as the spurious Issue of his Brain, and even cruelly denies it the common Privilege of his Name, struck with the delectable Beauty of it's Features, I could not avoid adopting the little *poetic Orphan*; and by dressing it up with a few Notes, &c. present it to the Public as perfect as possible.

Had I in Imitation of other great Authors, only consulted my Interest in the Publication of this inimitable Piece, (which doubtless will undergo numerous Impressions) I might first have sent it into the World *naked*, then by the Addition of a *Commentary*, *Notes Variorum*, *Prolegomena*, and all that, levy'd a new Tax upon the Public, and after all, by a Sort of modern poetical Legerdemain changing the *Name* of the *principal Hero*, and inserting a few *Hypercritics*, of a flattering Friend's, have render'd the former Editions incorrect, and couzen'd the curious Reader out of a *treble Consideration* for the *same Work*; but however this may suit the tricking Arts of a Bookseller, it is certainly much below the sublime Genius of an Author. — I know it will be said, that a Man has an equal Right to make as much as he can of his *Wit*, as well as of his *Money*; but then it ought to be consider'd, whether there may not be such a Thing as *Usury* in both, and the Law having only provided against

gainst

gainſt it in one Inſtance, is I apprehend no very moral Plea for the Practice of it in the other. *

The judicious Reader will eaſily perceive, that the following Poem in all its Properties partakes of the Epic; ſuch as fighting, ſpeeching, bullying, ranting, &c. (to ſay Nothing of the Moral) and as many thouſand Verſes are thought neceſſary to the Conſtruction of this Kind of Poem, it may be objected, that this is too *ſhort* to be rank'd under that Claſs; to which I ſhall only anſwer, that as *Conciſeneſs* is the laſt Fault a Writer is apt to *commit*, ſo it is generally the firſt a Reader is willing to *forgive*; and, tho' it may not be altogether ſo long, yet I dare ſay, it will not be found leſs replete with the true *Vis poetica*, than (not to mention the *Iliad, Æneid, &c.*) even *Leonidas* it-ſelf.

It may farther be objected, that the Characters of our principal Heros are too humble, for the Grandeur of the *Epic* Fable, but the candid Reader will be pleas'd to obſerve, that they are not here celebrated in their *mechanic*, but in their *heroic* Capacities, as *Boxers*, who by the Ancients themſelves, have ever been eſteem'd worthy to be immortaliz'd in the nobleſt Works of this Nature; of which the *Epeus* and *Euryalus* of *Homer*, and the *Entellus* and *Dares* of *Virgil* are inconteſtable Authorities. And as thoſe Authors were ever careful, that their princi-

B   cipal

---

* As this may be thought to be particularly aim'd at an *Author* who was lately reported to be dead, (and whoſe Loſs, all Lovers of the Muſes would have the greateſt Reaſon to lament) it may not be improper to aſſure the Reader, that it was written, and intended to have been publiſhed before that Report. and was only meant, as an Attack upon the *general* Abuſe of this Kind —— As to our Author himſelf, he has frequently given *public* Teſtimonies of his Veneration for that great Man's Genius, nor may it be unentertaining to the Reader, to acquaint him with one *private* Inſtance —— Immediately on hearing the Report of Mr *Pope*'s Death, he was heard to break forth in the following Exclamation.

POPE *dead!* —— *Huſh, Huſh* REPORT, *the ſlandrous Lye,*
FAME *ſays he lives,* —— *Immortals never die.*

cipal Perfonages, (however mean in themfelves) fhould derive their Pedigree from fome *Deity*, or illuftrious *Hero*, fo our Author has with equal Propriety made his fpring from *Phaëton*, and *Neptune*; under which Characters, he beautifully allegorizes their different Occupations of *Waterman*, and *Coachman*. — But for my own part, I cannot conceive, that the Dignity of the Hero's Profeffion, is any ways effential to that of the Action; *for if the greateft Perfons are guilty of the meaneft Actions, why may not the greateft Actions be afcrib'd to the meaneft Perfon.*

As the main Action of this Poem is entirely fupported by the principal Heros *themfelves*, it has been malicioufly infinuated to be defign'd, as an unmannerly Reflection on a *late glorious Victory*, where it is pretended, the whole Action was atchiev'd without the Interpofition of the principal Heros *at all* — But as the moft innocent Meanings may by ill Minds be wrefted to the moft wicked Purpofes, if any fuch Conftruction fhou'd be made, I will venture to affirm, that it muft proceed from the factious Venom of the Reader, and not from any difloyal Malignity in our Author, who is too well acquainted with the *Power*, ever to arraign the *Purity* of Government, befides the Poignance of the *Sword* is too prevalent for that of the *Pen*, and who, when there are at prefent, fo many thoufand *unanfwerable ftanding Arguments* ready to defend, wou'd ever be *Quixote* enough to attack, either the *Omnipotence* of a Prince, or the *Omnifcience* of his Minifters.

Were I to attempt an Analyfis of this Poem, I cou'd demonftrate that it contains (as much as a Piece of fo fublime a Nature will admit of) all thofe *true Standards* of Wit, Humour, Raillery, Satire, and Ridicule, which a late Writer has fo *marveloufly difcover'd*, and might on the Part of our Author fay with that profound Critic, —— *Jacta eft Alea*, but as the Obfcurity of a Beauty too ftrongly argues the Want of one, fo an Endeavour to elucidate the Merits of the following Performance, might be apt to give the Reader a difadvantageous Impreffion againft it, as it might tacitly imply, they were too myfterious to come within the Compafs of his Comprehenfion; I fhall therefore leave them to his more curious Obfervation, and bid him heartily Farewell —— *Lege & deleƐtare.*

SCRIBLERUS TERTIUS.

THE

THE
ARGUMENT
OF THE
FIRST BOOK.

*T*HE *Invocation, the Propofition, the Night before the Battle defcrib'd, the Morning opens, and difcovers the Multitude haffing to the Place of Action; their various Profeffions, Dignities, &c. illuftrated; the Spectators being feated, the youthful Combatants are firft introduc'd, their Manner of Fighting difplay'd; to thefe fucceed the Champions of a higher Degree, their fuperior Abilities mark'd, fome of the moft Eminent particularly celebrated; mean while, the principal Heroes are reprefented fitting, and ruminating on the approaching Combat, when the Herald fummons them to the Lifts.*

THE

THE
GYMNASIAD.
BOOK I.

SING, fing, O Mufe, the due contefted Fray,

And bloody Honours of that dreadful Day,

When *Phaeton*'s bold Son (tremendous Name)

Dar'd *Neptune*'s Off-fpring to the Lifts of Fame,

5 What Fury fraught Thee with Ambition's Fire,

Ambition, equal Foe to Son and Sire?

One,

V 3, 4. *When Phaeton's bold Son* ⎤ It is ufual for Poets to call the Sons
   Dared Neptune's Off-fpring. ⎦after the Names of their Fathers, as *A-gamemnon* the Son of *Atreus*, and *Achilles* the Son of *Peleus*, are frequently term'd *Pelides* and *Atrides*, our Author would doubtlefs have follow'd this laudable Example, but he found *Broughtonides* and *Stephenfonides*, or their Contractions, too unmufical for Metre, and therefore with wonderful Art adopts two poetical Parents, which obviates the Difficulty, and at the fame Time heightens the Dignity of his Heros.

          Bentleides.

   V 6. *Ambition equal Foe to Son and Sire.*⎤ It has been maintain'd by fome Philofophers, that the Paffions of the Mind are in fome meafure hereditary, as well as the Features of the Body, according to this Doctrine, our Author beautifully reprefents the Frailty of Ambition defcending from Father to Son, —— and as *Original Sin* may in fome Sort be accounted for on this Syftem, it is very probable our Author had a *theological*, as well as *phyfical*, and *moral* Meaning in this Verfe.

    For the latter Part of this Note, we are oblig'd to an *eminent Divine*.

One, hapless fell by *Jove*'s ætherial Arms,

And One, the *Triton*'s mighty Pow'r difarms.

Now all lay hush'd within the Folds of Night,

10 And faw in painted Dreams th' important Fight,

While Hopes and Fears alternate turn the Scales,

And now this Hero, and now that prevails;

Blows and imaginary Blood furvey,

Then waking, watch the flow Approach of Day.

15 When, lo! *Aurora* in her faffron Veft,

Darts a glad Ray, and gilds the ruddy Eaft.

Forth iffuing now all ardent feek the Place,

Sacred to Fame, and the Athletic Race;

As from their Hive the cluft'ring Squadrons pour,

20 O'er fragrant Meads to fip the vernal Flow'r;

So

So from each Inn the legal Swarms impel,

Of banded Seers, and Pupils of the Quill.

Senates and Shambles pour forth all their Store,

Mindful of Mutton, and of Laws no more,

25 E'en Money Bills, uncourtly, now muft wait,

And the fat Lamb has one more Day to bleat.

The Highway Knight now draws his Piftol's Load,

Refts his faint Steed, and this Day franks the Road.

Bailiffs,

V 21. *legal Swarms impel,*] An ingenious Critic of my Acquaintance obje&ed to this Simile, and would by no means admit, the Comparifon between *Bees* and *Lawyers* to be juft, *one*, he faid, was an induftrious, harmlefs, and ufeful Species, none of which Properties could be affirm'd of the *other*, and therefore he thought the *Drone* that lives on the Plunder of the Hive a more proper Archetype. I muft confefs myfelf in fome Meafure inclin'd to fubfcribe my Friend's Opinion, but then we muft confider, that our Author did not intend to defcribe their *Qualities*, but their *Number*, and in this Refpe& no one I think, can have any Obje&ion to the *Propriety* of the Comparifon.

V 24. *and of Laws no more*] The original M S has it, *Bribes*, but as this might feem to caft an invidious Afperfion on a certain Affembly, remarkable for their Abhorrence of Venality, and at the fame Time, might fubje& our Publifher to fome little Inconveniencies, I thought it prudent to foften the Expreffion, befides, I think this Reading renders our Author's Thought more natural, for tho' we fee the moft trifling Avocations are able to draw off their Attention from the *public Utility*, yet nothing is fufficient to divert a fteady Purfuit of their *private Emolument*

V 28 *this Day franks the Road*] Our Poet here artfully infinuates the Dignity of the Combat, he is about to celebrate, by it's being able to prevail on a Highwayman, to lay afide his Bufinefs to become a Spe&ator of it, —— and as, on this Occafion, he makes him forfake his *daily Bread* while the Senat r only negle&s the *Bufinefs of the Nation*, it may be obferv'd, how fatirically he gives the Preference in point of *Difinterefiednefs* to the Highway to

man

Bailiffs, in Crouds, neglect the dormant Writ,

30 And give another *Sunday* to the Wit,

He too would hie, but, ah! his Fortunes frown,

Alas! the fatal Pafsport's —— Half a Crown

Shoals prefs on Shoals, from Palace and from Cell,

Lords yeild the *Court*, and Butchers *Clerkenwell*.

35 St. *Giles*'s Natives, never known to fail,

All who have haply fcap'd th' obdurate Jail,

There many a martial Son of *Tott'nham* lyes,

Bound in *Devethan* Bands, a Sacrifice

To angry Juftice, nor muft view the Prize

40 Affembl'd Myriads croud the circling Seats,

High for the Combat every Bofom beats,

Each

V. 37 There many a martial Son, &c.] The unwary Reader may from this Paffage be apt to conclude, that an Amphitheatre is little better than a Nurfery for the Gallows, and that there is a Sort of phyfical Connection between *Boxing* and *Theiving*, but altho' Boxing may be a ufeful Ingredient in a Thief, yet it does not neceffarily make him one, Boxing is the Effect, not the Caufe, and Men are not *Thieves* becaufe they are *Boxers*, but *Boxers* becaufe they are *Thieves*. Thus Tricking, Lying, Evafion (with feveral other fuch like cardinal Virtues,) are a Sort of Properties pertaining to the Practice of the Law, as well as to the mercurial Profeffion. But would any one therefore infer that every *Lawyer* muft be a *Thief*.   *Scholiaft.*

Each Bosom partial for it's Hero bold,

Partial thro' Friendship, — or depending Gold.

But first, the infant Progeny of *Mars*

45 Join in the Lists, and wage their pigmy Wars;

Train'd to the manual Fight, and bruisful Toil,

The Stop defensive, and gymnastic Foil,

With nimble Fists their early Prowess shew,

And mark the future Hero in each Blow.

50 To these, the hardy iron-Race succeed,

All Sons of *Hockley* and fierce *Brickstreet* breed;

Mature in Valour, and inur'd to blood,

Dauntless each Foe in Form terrific stood;

C   Their

V. 44. *infant Progeny of Mars*] Our Author in this Description alludes to the *Lusus Trojæ* of *Virgil*,

> *Incedunt Pueri* ———————————————
> —————————— *Trojæ Juventus*
> —————— *Pugnæque ciunt simulachra sub armis.*

V 51. *Hockley and fierce Brickstreet Breed.*] Two famous Athletic Seminaries.

Their callous Bodies frequent in the Fray,

55 Mock'd the fell Stroke, nor to its Force gave way.

'Mongst thefe *Gloverius*, not the laft in Fame,

And he whofe Clog delights the beauteous Dame,

Nor leaft thy Praife whofe artificial Light,

In *Dian*'s Abfence gilds the Clouds of Night.

60 While thefe the Combat's direful Arts difplay,

And fhare the bloody Fortunes of the Day,

Each Hero fat, revolving in his Soul,

The various Means that might his Foe controul;

Conqueft and Glory each proud Bofom warms,

65 When, lo! the *Herald* fummon's them to Arms.

V 57 *And he whofe Clog* &c] Here we are prefented with a laudable Imitation of the ancient Simplicity of Manners, for as *Cincinnatus* difdain'd not the homely Employment of a *Ploughman*, fo we fee our Hero condefcending to the humble Occupation of a *Clog Maker*, and this is the more to be admir'd, as it is one Charaƈteriftic of modern Heroifm to be either above or below any Occupation at all

V. 58 *whofe artificial Light,*] Various and violent have been the Controverfies, whether our Author here intended to celebrate a *Lamp Lighter*, or a *Link-boy*, but as there are Heroes of both Capacities at prefent in the School of Honour, it is difficult to determine, whether the Poet alludes to a *Wells* or a *Buckhorfe.*

THE

THE
ARGUMENT
OF THE
SECOND BOOK.

STEPHENSON *enters the Lifts; a Defcription of his Figure; an Encomium on his Abilities, with refpect to the Character of Coachman.* Broughton *advances; his reverend Form defcrib'd; his fuperior Skill in the Management of the Lighter and Wherry difplay'd; his Triumph of the Badge celebrated; his Speech; his former Victories recounted; the Preparation for the Combat, and the Horror of the Spectators.* *

* *Argument*] It was doubtlefs in Obedience to 'Cuftom, and the Example of other great Poets, that our Author has thought proper to prefix an Argument to each Book, being minded that nothing fhould be wanting in the ufual Paraphernalia of Works of this Kind —— For my own Part, I am-at a Lofs to account for the Ufe of them, unlefs it be to fwell a Volume, or like Bills of Fare, to advertife the Reader what he is to expect, that if it contains nothing likely to fuit his Tafte, he may preferve his Appetite for the next Courfe.

BOOK

BOOK II.

FIRST, to the Fight, advanc'd the Charioteer,
High Hopes of Glory on his Brow appear;
Terror vindictive flashes from his Eye;
(To one the Fates the visual Ray deny)
5 Fierce glow'd his Looks, which spoke his inward Rage,
He leaps the Bar, and bounds upon the Stage.
The Roofs re-eccho with exulting Cries,
And all behold him with admiring Eyes.
Ill-fated Youth, what rash Desires could warm,
10 Thy manly Heart to dare the *Triton's* Arm?
Ah! too unequal to these martial Deeds,
Tho' none more skill'd to rule the foaming Steeds.
The Coursers still obedient to thy Rein,
Now urge their Flight, or now their Flight restrain.

Had

V. 6. 7. *He leaps the Bar, &c* ⎤ See the Descriptions of *Dares* in
The Roofs re-eccho   ⎦ *Virgl*

Nec mora, continuo vastis cum viribus effert
Ora Dares, magnoque virum se murmure tollit.

15 Had mighty *Diomed* provok'd the Race,

Thou far had'ſt left the *Grecian* in Diſgrace,

Where e'er you drove, each Inn confeſs'd your Sway,

Maids brought the Dram, and Oſtlers flew with Hay.

But know, tho' ſkill'd to guide the rapid Car,

20 None wages like thy Foe the manual War.

Now *Neptune*'s Offspring dreadfully ſerene,

Of Size gigantic, and tremendous Mein,

Steps forth, and 'midſt the fated Liſts appears,

Reverend his Form, but yet not worn with Years.

25 To him none equal in his youthful Day,

With feather'd Oar to ſkim the liquid Way;

Or thro' thoſe Streights whoſe Waters ſtun the Ear,

The loaded Lighter's bulky Weight to ſteer.

Soon.

V. 19 *But know tho' ſkill'd*] Here our Author inculcates a fine Moral by ſhewing how apt Men are to miſtake their Talents, but were Men only to act in their proper Spheres how often ſhould we ſee the *Parſon* in the Pew of the *Peaſant*, the *Author* in the Character of his *Hawker*, or a *Beau* in the Livery of his *Footman*, &c.

Soon as the Ring their ancient Warrior view'd,

30 Joy fill'd their Hearts, and thundring Shouts ensu'd;

Loud as when o'er *Thamesis'* gentle Flood,

Superior with the *Triton* Youths he row'd,

While far a-head his winged Wherry flew,

Touch'd the glad Shore, and claim'd the *Badge* its due.

35 Then thus indignant he accosts the Foe,

(While high Disdain sat prideful on his Brow.)

Long has the laurel Wreath victorious spread,

Its sacred Honours round this hoary Head;

The Prize of Conquest in each doubtful Fray,

40 And dear Reward of many a dire-fought Day.

Now

V. 34. the Badge its Due] A Prize given by Mr. *Dogget* to be annually contested on the first Day of *August*, —— as among the Ancients, *Games* and *Sports* were celebrated on mournful as well as joyful Events, there has been some Controversy whether our loyal *Comedian* meant the Compliment to the setting or rising Monarch of that Day, but as the Plate has a *Horse* for it's Device, I am induc'd to impute it to the latter, and, doubtless, he prudently consider'd, that as a living *Dog* is better than a dead *Lion*, the living *Horse* had, at least an equal Title to the same Preference.

Now Youth's cold Wane, the vigorous Pulfe has chas'd,

Froze all my Blood, and every Nerve unbrac'd,

Now, from thefe Temples fhall the Spoils be torn,

In fcornful Triumph by my Foe be worn?

45 What then avails my various Deeds in Arms,

If this proud Creft thy feeble Force difarms.

Loft be my Glories to recording Fame, .

When foil'd by Thee, the Coward blafts my Name, .

I who e'er Manhood my young Joints had knit,

50 Firft taught the fierce *Grettonius* to fubmit;

While drench'd in Blood, he proftrate prefs'd the Floor,

And inly groan'd the fatal Words —— *no more.*

Allenius too, who ev'ry Heart difmay'd,

Whofe Blows, like Hail, flew ratling round the Head;

Him

Ver 42. *Froze all my Blood,*] See *Virgil.*
—— *Sed enim gelidus tardante fenecta*
Sanguis hebet, frigentque effœtœ in corpore vires
V. 50 *Fierce* Grettonius *to fubmit* ,] *Gretton,* the moft famous Athleta,
in his Days, over whom our Heroe obtain'd his maiden Prize.
V. 53 *Allenius too,* &c.] Vulgarly known by the plebeian Name of
Pipes, which a learned Critic will have, to be derived from the Art and
Myftery of *Pipe-making,* in which it is affirm'd this Heroe was an Adept.
—— As he was the *Delicium pugnacis generis,* our Author, with marvellous
Judgment, reprefents the Ring weeping at his Defeat.
V. 54. *Whofe Blows like Hail,* &c] *Virgil*
—— *quam multa grandine nimbi*
Culminibus crepitant. ——

55 Him oft the Ring beheld with weeping Eyes,

Stretch'd on the Ground, reluctant yield the Prize.

Then fell the *Swain*, with whom none e'er could vie,

Where *Harrows* Steeple darts into the Sky.

Next the bold Youth a bleeding Victim lay,

60 Whose waving Curls the Barber's Art display.

You too this Arm's tremendous Prowess know,

Rash Man, to make this Arm again thy Foe.

This said —— the Heroes for the Fight prepare,

Brace their big Limbs and brawny Bodies bare.

65 The sturdy Sinews all aghast behold,

And ample Shoulders of *atlean* Mould;

Like

V. 57 *Then fell the* Swain] *Jeoffery Birch*, who in several Encounters, serv'd only to augment the Number of our Hero's Triumphs.

V. 59. *Next the bold Youth*] As this *Champion* is still living, and even disputes the Palm of Manhood with our Hero himself, I shall leave him to be the Subject of Immortality in some future *Gymnasiad*, should the Superiority of his Prowess, ever justify his Title to the *Corona Pugnea*.

V. 63. *This said,* &c] *Virgil.*

> *Hæc fatus, duplicem ex Humeris rejecit Amictum;*
> *Et magnos Membrorum Artus, magna ossa lacertosque*
> *Exuit.*

Like *Titan*'s Offspring who 'gainſt Heav'n ſtrove,

So each, tho' mortal, ſeem'd a Match for *Jove*.

Now round the Ring a ſilent Horror reigns,

Speechleſs each Tongue, and bloodleſs all their Veins.

70 When lo! the Champions give the dreadful Sign,

And Hand in Hand in friendly Token join;

Thoſe iron Hands, which ſoon upon the Foe,

With giant force, muſt deal the deathful Blow.

D   THE

THE
ARGUMENT
OF THE
THIRD BOOK.

A Description of the Battle; Stephenson *is van-quished*; *the* Manner *of his* Body *being carried off by his* Friends; Broughton *claims the* Prize, *and takes his final* Leave *of the* Stage.

BOOK

BOOK III.

FULL in the Center now they fix in Form,

Eye meeting Eye, and Arm oppos'd to Arm;

With wily Feints each other now provoke,

And cautious meditate th' impending Stroke.

5 Th' impatient Youth infpir'd by Hopes of Fame,

First fped his Arm, unfaithful to its Aim;

The wary Warrior watchful of his Foe,

Bends back, and fcapes the death-defigning Blow;

With erring Glance it founded by his Ear,

10 And whizzing fpent its idle Force in Air.

Then quick advancing on the unguarded Head,

A dreadful Show'r of Thunderbolts he fhed;

D 2

As

V 7, 8. ———— *watchful of his Foe,*
   Bends back, and fcapes the Death defigning Blow,] *Virgil*
   ———— *ille Ictum venientem a vertice velox*
   Prævidit, celerique elapfus corpore ceffit.

V. 10 *its idle Force in Air*] *Idem*
   ———-- *vires in ventum effudit* ————

As when a Whirlwind from some cavern broke,

With furious Blasts assaults the monarch Oak,

15 This way and that its lofty Top it bends,

And the fierce Storm the crackling Branches rends.

So wav'd the Head, and now to left and right,

Rebounding flies, and crash'd beneath the weight.

Like the young Lion wounded by a Dart,

20 Whose Fury kindles at the galling smart;

The Heroe rouzes with redoubled Rage,

Flies on his Foe, and foams upon the Stage.

Now grapling, both in close Contention join,

Legs lock in Legs, and Arms in Arms entwine;

They

V 19 *Like the young Lion*] It may be observ'd, that our Author has treated the Reader but with one Simile throughout the two foregoing Books, but in order to make him ample Amends, has given him no less than six in this. Doubtless this was in Imitation of *Homer*, and artfully intended to heighten the Dignity of the main Action, as well as our Admiration towards the Conclusion of his Work —— *Finis coronat Opus.*

V 24 *Arms in Arms entwine,*] *Virgil*
    Immiscentque manus manibus, pugnamque lacessunt.

25 They fweat, they heave, each tugging Nerve they ftrain,

 Both fix'd as Oaks, their fturdy Trunks fuftain.

 At length the Chief his wily Art difplay'd,

 Poiz'd on his Hip the haplefs Youth he laid;

 Aloft in Air his quiv'ring Limbs he throw'd,

30 Then on the Ground down dafh'd the pondrous Load.

 So fome vaft Ruin on a mountain's Brow,

 Which tott'ring hangs, and dreadful nods below,

 When the fierce Tempeft the Foundation rends,

 Whirl'd thro' the Air with horrid Crufh defcends.

35 Bold and undaunted up the Hero rofe,

 Fiercer his Bofom for the Combat glows,

 Shame ftung his manly Heart, and fiery Rage

 New fteel'd each Nerve, redoubl'd War to wage.

Swift

V. 35. *Bold and undaunted,* &c] *Virgil.*

> *At non tardatus Cafu, neque territus Heros,*
> *Acrior ad pugnam redit, & Vim fufcitat Ira.*
> *Tum Pudor incendit Vires ————*

Swift to revenge the dire Difgrace he flies,

40 Again fufpended on the Hip he lies;

Dafh'd on the Ground, again had fatal fell,

Haply the Barrier caught his flying Heel;

There faft it hung, th' imprifon'd Head gave way,

And the ftrong Arm defrauded of its Prey.

45 Vain ftrove the Chief to whirl the Mountain o'er,

It flipt —— he headlong rattles on the Floor.

Around the Ring loud Peals of Thunder rife,

And Shouts exultant eccho to the Skies.   Uplifted

V. 42 Haply the Barrier, &c] Our Author, like *Homer* himfelf, is no lefs to be admir'd in the Character of an Hiftorian than in that of a Poet, we fee him here faithfully reciting the moft minute Incidents of the Battle, and in-forming us, that the youthful Hero being on the Lock, muft again inevitably have come to the Ground had not his Heel catch'd the Bar, and that his Antagonift by the Violence of his ftraining, flipt his Arm over his Head, and by that Means receiv'd the Fall he intended the Enemy. —— I thought it incumbent on me as a Commentator to fay thus much, to illuftrate the Meaning of our Author, which might feem a little obfcure to thofe who are unacquainted with Conflicts of this Kind.

V. 48 eccho to the Skies, &c] *Virgil.*
          It Clamor Cœlo ————————

The learned Reader will perceive our Author's frequent Allufions to *Virgil,* and whether he intended them as Tranflations or Imitations of the *Roman* Poet, muft give us Paufe, but as in our modern Productions, we find, *Imitations* are generally nothing more than *bad Tranflations,* and *Tranflations* nothing more than *bad Imitations,* it would equally I fuppofe fatisfie the Gall of the Critic, fhould thefe unluckily fall within either Defcription.

Uplifted now inanimate he seems,

50 Forth from his Nostrils gush the purple Streams;

Gasping for Breath, and impotent of Hand,

The Youth beheld his Rival stag'ring stand.

But he alas! had felt th' unnerving Blow,

And gaz'd unable to assault the Foe.

55 As when two Monarchs of the brindl'd Breed,

Dispute the proud Dominion of the Mead,

They fight, they foam, then wearied in the Fray,

Aloof retreat, and low'ring stand at Bay.

So stood the Heros, and indignant glar'd,

60 While grim with Blood their rueful Fronts were smear'd,

Till with returning Strength new Rage returns,

Again their Arms are steel'd, again each Bosom burns.

Incessant now their Hollow Sides they pound,

Loud on each Breast the bounding Bangs resound,   Their

V. 63. Incessant now, &c.] *Virg.l.*
> *Multa Viri nequicquam inter Se vulnere jactant*
> *Multa cavo lateri ingeminant & pectore vastos*
> *Dant sonitus, erratque aures & tempora circum*
> *Crebra manus, duro crepitant sub vulnere Malæ*

65 Their flying Fists around the Temples glow,

And the Jaws crackle with the maffy Blow.

The raging Combat ev'ry Eye appals,

Strokes following Strokes, and Falls fucceeding Falls.

Now droop'd the Youth, yet urging all his Might,

70 With feeble Arm ftill vindicates the Fight.

Till on the part where heav'd the panting Breath,

A fatal Blow imprefs'd the Seal of Death.

Down dropt the Hero, welt'ring in his Gore,

And his ftretch'd Limbs lay quiv'ring on the Floor.

75 So when a Faulcon fkims the airy way,

Stoops from the Clouds, and pounces on his Prey;

Dafh'd on the earth the feather'd Victim lies,

Expands its feeble wings, and, flutt'ring, dies.

His faithful Friends their dying Hero rear'd,

80 O'er his broad Shoulders dangling hung his Head;

Dragging

V. 79 *His faithful Friends*] *Virgil.*
  Aft illum fidi Æquales, genua ægra trahentem,
  Jactantemque utroque caput, craffumque cruorem
  Ore ejectantem, miftofque ic fanguine dentes,
  Ducunt ad naves——————

Dragging its Limbs, they bear the Body forth,

Mash'd Teeth and clotted Blood came issuing from his Mouth.

Thus then the Victor ——— O cœlestial Pow'r!

Who gave this Arm to boast one Triumph more,

85 Now grey in Glory, let my Labours cease.

My blood-stain'd Laurel wed the Branch of Peace,

Lur'd by the Lustre of the golden Prize,

No more in Combat this proud Crest shall rise,

To future Heros future Deeds belong,

90 Be mine the Theme of some immortal Song.

This said ---- he seiz'd the Prize, while round the Ring.

High soar'd Applause on Acclamations Wing.

V 88. *No more in Combat,* &c.] *Idem*
——— *hic Victor cœstus, artemque repono.*

F I N I S.

CPSIA information can be obtained at www.ICGtesting.com
Printed in the USA
BVOW05s1055081015

421591BV00016B/217/P